Written by
Traci Ferguson Geiser

Editors: Carla Hamaguchi and Heather Butler
Illustrator: Jenny Campbell
Cover Illustrator: Rick Grayson
Designer/Production: Moonhee Pak/Cari Helstrom
Cover Designer: Barbara Peterson
Art Director: Tom Cochrane
Project Director: Carolea Williams

Table of Contents

Introduction

Picture books open the imagination. They excite and inspire children. What better way to illustrate key reading skills than through cherished picture books? These read-alouds engage children in learning how our language works. Research has shown that effective reading programs must include instruction in five areas: *phonemic awareness, phonics, vocabulary, fluency,* and *comprehension.* The aim of this book is to use the friendly, engaging format of picture books to combine instruction in the five key areas of a complete primary reading program. A summary of these areas of instruction follows.

When children first hear words, they process them as whole sounds. Words like *milk, more, no, up,* and *mommy* are heard as one unit. Phonemic awareness instruction helps children notice, manipulate, and consider the individual sounds words are comprised of. Phonemic awareness instruction exposes children to phonemes, or speech sounds, and prepares them to learn about the corresponding letter symbols in phonics. Phonemic awareness instruction should include the following:

- **Phoneme Isolation**—Children recognize individual sounds in a word.
    Teacher: *What is the first sound in* **van***?*
    Children: *The first sound in* **van** *is* /v/.
- **Phoneme Identification**—Children recognize the same sound in different words.
    Teacher: *What sound is the same in* **fix, fall,** *and* **fun***?*
    Children: *The first sound,* /f/, *is the same.*
- **Phoneme Categorization**—Children recognize the word in a set of three or four words that has the "odd" sound.
    Teacher: *Which word doesn't belong?* **Bus, bun,** *or* **rug***?*
    Children: **Rug** *does not belong. It doesn't begin with* /b/.

- **Phoneme Blending**—Children listen to a sequence of separately spoken phonemes and then combine the phonemes to form a word. Then they write and read the word.
    Teacher: *What word is* /b/ /i/ /g/?
    Children: /b/ /i/ /g/ *is* **big**.
    Teacher: *Now let's write the sounds in* **big***:* /b/, *write* **b***;* /i/, *write* **i***;* /g/, *write* **g***.* (Write **big** on the board.) *Now we're going to read the word* **big***.*
- **Phoneme Segmentation**—Children break a word into its separate sounds, saying each sound as they tap it out or count it. Then they write and read the word.
    Teacher: *How many sounds are in* **grab***?*
    Children: /g/ /r/ /a/ /b/. *Four sounds.*
    Teacher: *Now let's write the sounds in* **grab***:* /g/, *write* **g***;* /r/, *write* **r***;* /a/, *write* **a***;* /b/, *write* **b***.* (Write **grab** on the board.) *Now we're going to read the word* **grab***.*
- **Phoneme Deletion**—Children recognize a new word when a phoneme is removed.
    Teacher: *What is* **smile** *without the* /s/?
    Children: **Smile** *without the* /s/ *is* **mile**.
- **Phoneme Addition**—Children make a new word by adding a phoneme to an existing word.
    Teacher: *What word do you have if you add* /s/ *to the beginning of* **park***?*
    Children: **Spark**.

- **Phoneme Substitution**—Children substitute one phoneme for another to make a new word.
  Teacher: *The word is* **bug**. *Change /g/ to /n/. What's the new word?*
  Children: **Bun**.

Phonics

Phonics connects the sounds of language to the written symbols that represent them. Phonics instruction helps children learn these relationships and begin to understand the alphabetic principle—the predictable patterns of written letters and spoken sounds. Phonics instruction must be systematic and explicit to be effective. That is, phonics instruction must follow a logical sequence that introduces the most common and simple relationships first and builds in complexity. It must be presented clearly and with specific, measurable objectives. Phonics instruction is not always intuitive. In addition, effective phonics instruction includes the opportunity, on an ongoing basis, for children to apply the new skills they're learning to words, sentences, and larger pieces of text.

Vocabulary

There are two basic types of vocabulary: *receptive* (vocabulary a child understands when he or she hears it) and *expressive* (vocabulary a child uses when speaking). Both need to be developed for a child to read well. However, when studying how children acquire and use vocabulary, it's more helpful to think in terms of spoken and written vocabulary. Beginning readers lean heavily on their knowledge of spoken vocabulary to decode new words they encounter in text—whether or not they actually

use those words in conversation. It is much more difficult for a child to decode a new word he or she has not heard. As children develop their reading skills, they also develop their written vocabulary. Children cannot understand texts that contain an unreasonable number of unfamiliar words. The following are six teaching strategies to help foster vocabulary development:

- **Preteaching Vocabulary**—Before reading a story, teach children words that they may find difficult to read or understand. This should include words important to the story, words with multiple meanings or spellings, and idioms.
- **Using Context Clues**—Children use illustrations, other words in the sentence, and surrounding sentences to decode an unknown word.
- **Repeated Exposure**—Children are introduced to a new word and are then given many situations to hear and use the word over time.
- **Extended Instruction**—Children are given extended instruction and activities to reinforce and practice the new words.
- **Using Reference Books**—Children are taught strategies to figure out the pronunciation and meaning of new words.
- **Using Word Parts**—Children take a word and break it into parts to decipher meaning (e.g., prefixes, suffixes, compound words).

Fluency

Fluency instruction may seem cosmetic on the surface. Its aim is to produce a reader who sounds natural while reading. Fluent readers are accurate, quick, and able to read with expression. They make the reading sound interesting. But beyond enhancing the experience for listeners, fluent readers are also demonstrating skills that are crucial to their understanding of what they read. Fluent readers recognize words at a glance, group words into meaningful phrases, and move beyond the struggle to decode individual words. They are able to focus on making sense of what they read. Fluency is often the missing bridge between being able to "read" a text and being able to understand it. Readers who decode word-by-word sound plodding and choppy. And worse, they are too busy to have time to think about what they are reading as they read it. The most effective way to encourage fluency in children is to model it and to provide children with frequent opportunities to read aloud. Children who know you are listening for fluency are often motivated to read more fluently.

Comprehension

Comprehension instruction helps children to understand what they read, to remember it, and to be able to communicate with others about what they read. Children who have a reason for reading a piece beyond its role as an assignment (e.g., I'm going to find out how bats see in the dark) are more likely to show a higher degree of comprehension when they have completed the reading. The process of comprehension is a complicated one, involving the use of a number of skills, including those already mentioned. One of the most important aspects of comprehension is children's ability to know when they do not understand what they are reading. Good readers know when their own comprehension has broken down. Research has identified five effective techniques that you can teach children in order to improve their comprehension skills:

- **Monitoring Comprehension**—Teach children to be aware of what they do and don't understand (metacognition) and to be willing to solve problems in comprehension as they occur.
- **Using Graphic Organizers**—Graphic organizers help children filter out the unimportant details and focus on the story structure and relationships. They also help children craft well-organized summaries.
- **Answering Questions**—Children answer the teacher's questions, both literal (facts explicitly stated in the text) and inferential (involving making connections or inferences from the text).
- **Generating Questions**—Children generate questions from the text. Initially, they focus on literal or explicit questions. Over time, they will model their questions on the questions the teacher asks of them.
- **Summarizing**—Summarizing involves children processing the key points in the text and explaining those points in their own words.

How to Use This Book

This book is designed to provide teachers with an easy guide to cover the five key areas of reading instruction while reading popular literature selections.

Skills Taught

This section (see page 8) provides a dot chart of the skills taught with each literature selection. This is a quick resource to find which lessons teach a specific skill. Refer to this list when your class needs added emphasis in one of these areas.

General Activity Ideas

This section (starting on page 9) includes activity ideas for each of the five key areas of reading instruction. These activities can be used with any literature selection. Choose one of these activities when you feel your children need a little more practice in a given area. These can be used in addition to the activities provided for each literature selection. You will also find included in this section a Character Map reproducible and a Story Sequence reproducible, as well as two lists of sample questions—Questions to Ask Readers and Questions Good Readers Ask.

Activities for Literature Selections

There are five activities to accompany each literature selection. Read aloud the literature selection. Then have children complete each activity. Depending on your class, you can spread the activities over the course of a week, do a couple of activities per day, or do all the activities in one day.

Phonics Reproducibles

For each phonics activity, there is a student reproducible page to provide children with more practice. These pages can be reproduced and sent home for

homework to reinforce the phonics lesson, or you can have children work independently on them in class.

Read-Around Reproducibles

Since most of the literature selections will not be at the appropriate reading level for your children to read independently, an activity called "Read-Around" has been provided with each literature selection. Each reproducible has six cards on a page. The cards contain phrases with spaces between groups of words so children can see and better understand how to read words in groups. The phrases on the cards are short and simple to help children focus directly on reading phrases and practicing high-frequency and content words. Each card has at least one content word from the literature selection. As an extension, invite children to take home a set of cards. Have them teach their family how to play so they can practice reading the cards with family members.

Read-Around Directions

1 Make multiple copies (each page is a set of six cards for a group) of the Read-Around from the desired literature selection, and cut apart the cards.

2 Give a set to a small group of children so that each child has one to three cards. Review with children the pronunciation and meaning of the boldfaced words on their cards so that they are comfortable with those key words. The boldfaced words are from the literature selection.

3 Read aloud each child's cards, and then have children silently read their cards at least five times to build fluency.

4 Explain that children will play a listening and reading game. Model how the game works. Explain that each child will be listening for a portion of the first line of words on his or her card to be read aloud. That child will then read aloud his or her entire card, pausing at the spaces, and wait for the next child to answer.

5 Tell the group that the child who has the card that says *I have the first card* will begin the game by reading aloud his or her card. Tell children to continue the game until they get back to the first card. (The game ends after a child reads *Who has the first card?* and a child answers *I have the first card.*)

6 Encourage children to play the game at least twice. Have children mix up the cards and pass them out again so that children read different cards each time.

Literature Selections

A list of the literature selections used in this book is provided on page 80 in a convenient reference format, which includes authors and publishers.

Read-Around

I have the first card. Who has the word **hand**?
I have the word **hand**. Who has the word **kiss**?
I have the word **kiss**. Who has the word **warm**?
I have the word **warm**. Who has the word **love**?
I have the word **love**. Who has the word **home**?
I have the word **home**. Who has the first card?

The Kissing Hand **23**

Read-Around

I have the first card. Who has the **brown winter tree**?
I have the **brown winter tree**. Who has the **wind**?
I have the **wind**. Who has the **bird nests**?
I have the **bird nests**. Who has the **apples**?
I have the **apples**. Who has the **apple pie**?
I have the **apple pie**. Who has the first card?

The Apple Pie Tree **27**

Skills Taught

Skill	The Kissing Hand	The Apple Pie Tree	Red Leaf, Yellow Leaf	Where the Wild Things Are	Corduroy	Stone Soup	The Snowy Day	Froggy Gets Dressed	The Mitten	Arthur's Valentine	Tacky the Penguin	Big Red Barn	Guess How Much I Love You	The Relatives Came	The Rainbow Fish
Phonemic Awareness															
Phoneme Isolation		•					•								
Phoneme Identification					•										•
Phoneme Categorization			•												
Phoneme Blending	•							•				•			
Phoneme Segmentation										•					
Phoneme Deletion											•				
Phoneme Addition				•		•								•	
Phoneme Substitution									•			•			
Phonics															
Long and Short Vowels				o	i						e				
ee			•												
Consonant Digraphs	sh								wh	ch sh				th	
Consonant Blends															sw
Plural s		•													
Consonant Sounds						/s/ /z/		/z/							
-ing Ending							•								
Word Families											-ay		-own		
Vocabulary															
Preteaching Vocabulary						•	•					•		•	
Using Context Clues				•					•						
Repeated Exposure	•									•		•			•
Extended Instruction					•										
Using Reference Books		•						•					•		
Using Word Parts			•												
Comprehension															
Monitoring Comprehension												•		•	
Using Graphic Organizers							•	•			•				
Answering Questions	•			•			•		•				•		
Generating Questions			•		•					•			•		
Summarizing		•													•

 # General Activity Ideas

Phonemic Awareness

Students need to have a strong understanding of spoken language before they can understand written language. This knowledge of how language works is called *phonemic awareness*. Phonemic awareness is the ability to examine language independent of meaning (i.e., hear the sounds that make up the words), attend to sounds in the context of a word (i.e., see relationships between sounds), and manipulate sounds (i.e., alter and rearrange sounds to create new words). The following are phonemic awareness activities that can be used with any literature selection.

Punch It Out (Phoneme Isolation)

Focus on target ending sounds by having children use hand motions as they say words. First, say a word from a literature book (e.g., *cat*) without using hand motions. Repeat the word and add hand motions. Slide your hand (palm down) from left to right as you say the word, and then thrust a fist to "punch out" the last sound (/t/). Have children repeat the word and hand motions. Repeat the activity with other words from the book.

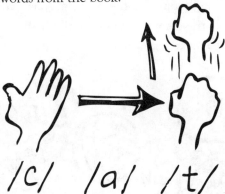

One, Two, or Three? (Phoneme Isolation)

Tell children that you will say a word from the literature selection and that they will listen to hear what sound is at the beginning of the word. Explain that you will then give them three choices and that they should hold up the correct number of fingers to indicate which choice matches the sound they

heard at the beginning of the word. For your first example, say *The first word is **cat***. *Which sound do you hear at the beginning?* /t/? *(Hold up one finger.)* /k/? *(Hold up two fingers.)* Or /a/? *(Hold up three fingers.)* Children should hold up two fingers. Continue the activity with other words from the book. Repeat the activity, asking children to identify the middle or ending sounds.

Pop-up People (Phoneme Blending)

Have volunteers sit in the front of the class. Secretly tell each one a beginning, middle, or ending sound of a word, such as /m/, /a/, or /t/. Have volunteers sit in the correct order; then have them "pop up" one at a time saying their sound. Ask the rest of the class to blend the sounds together and guess the word. Repeat the activity with other words and volunteers.

Thumbs Up! (Phoneme Identification)

Give each child a smiley face sticker to place on his or her thumb. Select a target sound such as /d/. Tell children to give a "smiley thumbs up" signal each time they hear the target sound at the beginning of a word. Read a literature selection; invite children to indicate each time they hear the sound.

Book Look (Phoneme Substitution)

Read a literature book with rhyming text to the class. Then close the book, and repeat some of the lines, leaving off the final rhyming word. For example, you might say *Would you like them in a house? Would you like them with a _____.* (mouse) Have children provide the missing word. After children have provided the rhyming word, repeat the same sentence, and ask children to think of other words that would work with the sentence. For example, *Not in a box. Not with _____.* (some clocks)

Blending with Chalk
(Phoneme Segmentation and Blending)

Choose a word from the literature book, say it normally, and then break it up into individual phonemes. Have children draw on the chalkboard a circle for each phoneme they hear. For example, for the word *jump,* they would draw four circles. Have children touch each circle with their chalk and repeat the individual phonemes for the word (e.g., /j/ /u/ /m/ /p/). Have them take a tissue and gently smear the chalk circles from left to right

while slowly blending the phonemes to make the word. Have children repeat the smear faster while blending the phonemes again at a closer to normal speed. Finally, as they erase the circles from left to right, have them say the word at normal speed. Repeat the activity with other words from the book.

Final Phoneme Substitution
(Phoneme Substitution)

Have children sit in a circle. Hold up a large playground ball, and explain that the child you toss the ball to will have to change the last sound he or she hears in the word you name to make a new word. Say *For example, I am going to start with the word* **map**. **Map** *is made of /m/ /a/ /p/. What sound can I use to make a word with /mmmmmaaaa/ instead of /p/?* Have children brainstorm until they have come up with several possibilities. Explain that if a child thinks of a new ending, he or she may choose any other child to throw the ball to. If the child cannot think of a word, he or she has to call on a child who raises his or her hand to supply a correct answer. The child with the first correct answer gets the ball. If no child can think of a real word with a new ending, supply another word to start over with. Continue the game until every child has had a chance to make a new word.

Phonics

Phonics instruction aims to teach children that there are predictable patterns and relationships between letters and spoken sounds. When children understand these patterns and relationships, they recognize known words faster and decode new words more effectively. They read new words better in isolation and in context. The most effective methods of phonics instruction offer direct instruction of specific letter-sound relationships in a logical sequence. Systematic phonics instruction is effective in improving word recognition and spelling in kindergarten and first grade. Phonics instruction must be progressive and specific to be effective, and must provide opportunities for children to use new information in a meaningful context. Because a sequential and complete phonics program is beyond the scope of this book, the activities for phonics are meant to supplement your existing phonics program.

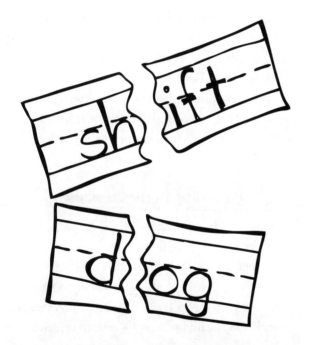

Learning Ring

Cut several sentence strips into small strips of the same length. Place ten strips in a stack, and hole-punch the left side of each strip. Use a binder ring to attach the strips together. On the top strip, write a letter-sound relationship (e.g., *ea*) that children have recently studied. Then write words that include the target letter-sound relationship (e.g., *beat*, *seat*) on the other strips. Place the rings at a center, divide the class into pairs, and give each pair of children a ring of words. Have one partner flip through the cards and read each word to the other partner. Then have children switch reader/listener roles.

Word Puzzles

Choose words from a literature selection. Write each word on a sentence strip. Then divide the word between two phonemes by cutting the sentence strip apart—using an interesting cut. The finished cards should function like a jigsaw puzzle in that there should be only one "match" for each card. Shuffle all of the card pieces, and give one piece to each child. Challenge children to find the child with the card that matches their card. When partners find each other, they should read their word together. Then have each pair read their word to the class.

Vocabulary

Children learn most of their vocabulary through indirect methods. They hear a given word over and over in different contexts. Initially, this builds recognition, and over time, it leads to a more complete understanding of the word's meaning. Only a small portion of a child's vocabulary is gained through direct instruction, but it is still an important part of vocabulary acquisition. Here are some vocabulary activity ideas.

Act It Out

Write a vocabulary word on the board, and read it aloud. If the word is a noun, use gestures to show typical size and shape. Pantomime how the item is used, showing how much effort it might take to use it, its relative weight, and expressions that show how enjoyable the experience is or is not. If the word is a verb, pantomiming can provide children with a memorable level of understanding. Use pantomime to illustrate an adjective by showing how something is changed by it or responds to it. For example, you might demonstrate *windy* by pantomiming trying to walk outside on a blustery day, losing your hat, and leaning into the wind.

Role-Play

List the vocabulary words on the board, and discuss their meanings with the class. Divide the class into small groups, and assign each group one of the vocabulary words. Ask each group to create a skit in which they use the word at least three times. Have one child in each group hold up a sign with the printed word each time the word is used in the skit.

Picture Walk

Show children the cover of a literature book. Discuss with children the title of the book. Ask them to predict what the book will be about. Do a "picture walk" through the story. Have children suggest words that describe each picture. When you come to a page with a word that children suggested, point to that word and say *Look, the author used that word, too.* Track the word with your finger while reading it aloud. Then write the word on the board. After you have completed the picture walk, refer to the list of vocabulary words on the board, and discuss the meaning of each word with children.

Use Words in Context

Challenge children to use a vocabulary word in context for the next week after the word is introduced. Keep a tally of each time a child uses the word correctly. At the end of the week, count the tallies. If the class gets ten tally marks at the end of the week, every child receives a reward or prize.

Fluency

There are a number of strategies that can be applied in the classroom and at home to maximize opportunities for coaching readers as they read aloud. When you provide a child with fluency instruction and practice, reading material should be at his or her independent reading level. No more than 1 in 20 words should be unfamiliar. Some suggested methods are summarized below.

Model Fluent Reading

Read aloud to your class daily. Model expression and pacing as you read. Occasionally, stop and point out what you are doing and why. For example, you might say *Did you notice how my voice paused after the words* **tiny mouse**? (Point to the words.) *That is because there is a comma there, and a comma tells me to pause for a moment.*

Children Read Aloud Modeled Text

After you model how to read the text, provide repeated opportunities for children to read the same material. Some experiences should be whole group and some should be individual. The following methods are six ways to provide children with these experiences:

- **Student-Adult Reading**—Invite adults (parents, teachers, or other staff) to your classroom to read one-on-one with each child. Have the adults read aloud first; then have the children read while the adults assist with any reading difficulties. Invite children to reread the story several times until it can be read fluently. This should take approximately three to four rereadings.

- **Tape-Assisted Reading**—Children read along in their book as they hear a fluent reader read the book on an audiotape. Use a tape recorder to record yourself or another adult reading the text at a pace of approximately 80 to 100 words per minute. Model intonation and pacing. The tape should not have sound effects or music. For the first reading, ask the child to follow along with the tape, pointing to each word in his or her book as the reader reads it. Next, have the child try to read aloud with the tape. Reading along with the tape should continue until the child is able to read the book independently, without the support of the tape.

- **Choral Reading** — Read aloud to children to model fluent reading. Ask children to follow along in their own book as you reread it to them. Invite them to join in when you come to a word they know. As you read the book a third time, encourage children to read aloud with you. Children should read the book with you three to five times total (though not necessarily on the same day). By this time, children should be able to read the text independently.

- **Small-Group Reading** — Children read together as a group, with an adult. Practice should be provided three to five times. Print needs to be large enough for the whole group to see, or each child needs his or her own copy of the text. Have the adult read the first two or three pages of text to model fluent reading. Have children read aloud the remaining text in turns or together.

- **Partner Reading** — Place children in pairs; more-fluent readers can be paired with less-fluent readers. Have the stronger reader read aloud a page first to provide a model of fluent reading. Then ask the less-fluent reader to read aloud the same text. The stronger child can assist with word recognition and provide feedback and encouragement to the less-fluent partner. Have the less-fluent partner reread the passage aloud until he or she can read it independently. Partner reading can also be done by pairing children who read at the same level to reread a story that you have previously read to the class. Ask each partner to take turns reading to each other several times until they are both able to read the story fluently. Have children take their books home to read to their families.

- **Reader's Theater** — In Reader's Theater, children rehearse and perform a play for an audience. Provide children with a script that has been derived from a book that is rich in dialogue. Have children play characters who speak lines or a narrator who shares necessary background information. Reader's Theater provides readers with a legitimate reason to reread text and to practice fluency. It also promotes cooperative interaction with peers and makes the reading task appealing.

Comprehension

Regardless of the purpose for reading—enjoyment or gathering information—it cannot be fulfilled if children do not comprehend what they read. If children can decode the words but do not understand the text, they are not really reading. Listed below are activities to help children improve their comprehension skills.

Monitoring Comprehension

Before reading a book to the class, tell children that you would like them to raise their hand if they have questions about anything in the story as you read it. As children ask their questions, have the rest of the class give their feedback to help answer any questions that arise. If children are unable to answer a question, you may answer it for them or consult the book, a dictionary, or other reference aid for help. Once all of the questions have been answered, reread the story.

Using Graphic Organizers

Give each child a Character Map reproducible (page 16). Have children write in the center circle the name of one character. Then ask them to draw inside the remaining circles the pictures that describe the character. More-fluent writers can write short phrases in the circles instead of drawing pictures.

Answering Questions

Read aloud a literature selection. At various places in the reading, stop and ask children questions. Do not ask more than a few questions at each stop since the emphasis should not shift from the primary goal—reading. Ask questions that require

children to connect in different ways what they know and what they are reading. See page 17 for a list of sample questions.

Generating Questions

Encourage children to ask questions of themselves and their peers, similar in nature and sophistication to the questions you have been asking of them. Challenge children to connect ideas from different sections of the text when they create questions. Encourage them to go beyond the literal fact-finding questions. See page 18 for a list of questions that good readers ask.

Summarizing

Read aloud a story, and ask children to listen for the events that make up the beginning, middle, and end of the story. Give each child a Story Sequence reproducible (page 19). Have children draw a picture of what happened in the beginning, middle, and end of the story. Ask your class to help you write on chart paper a summary of the story using the Story Sequence reproducible as a guide. Remind children that summaries should be brief. Help children condense their sentences, if necessary, before writing them on the chart paper.

Character Map

Date _____

Name _____

Character's Name

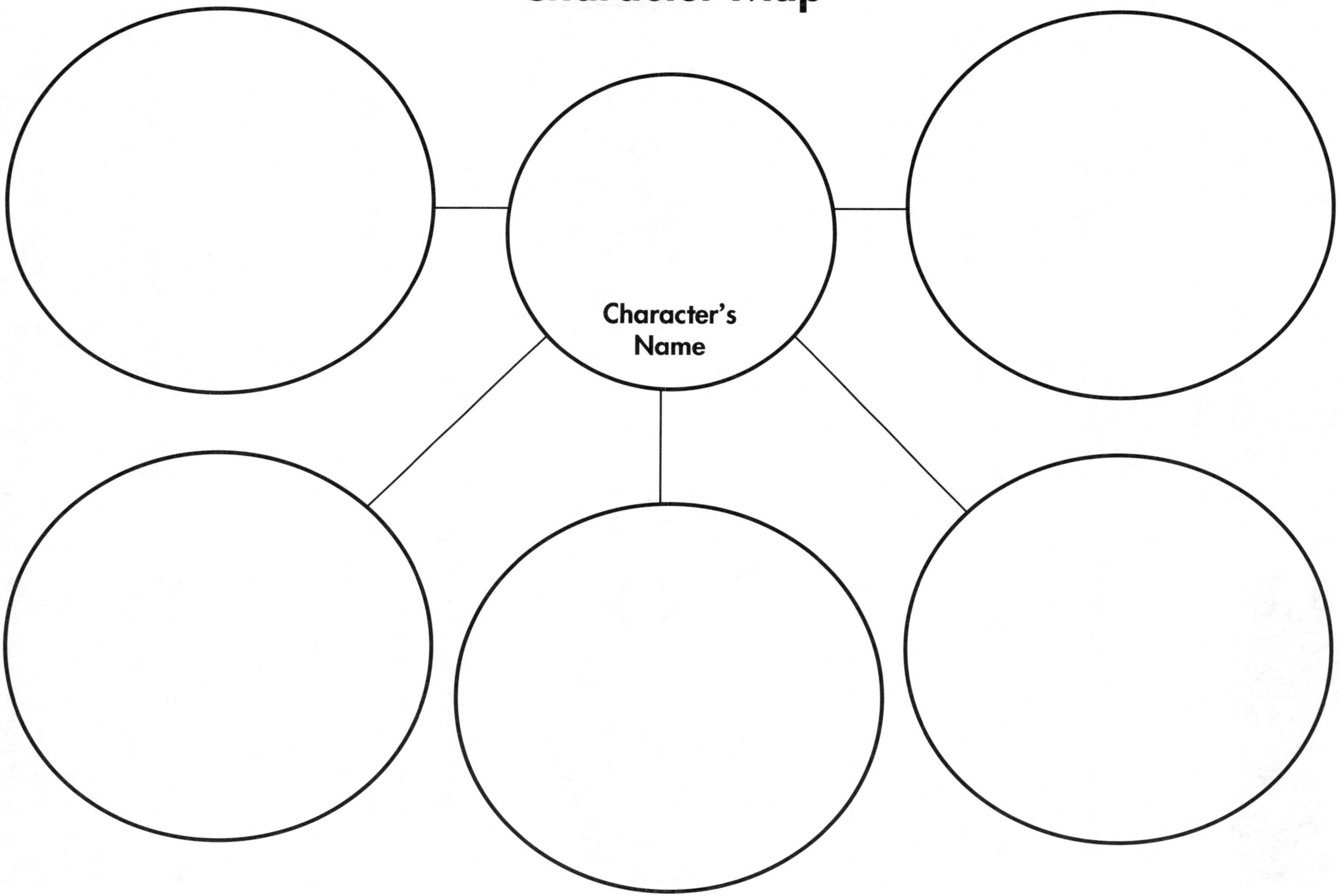

Teaching Reading Using Picture Books • *K–1* © 2005 Creative Teaching Press

Questions to Ask Readers

Questions That Connect (i.e., that connect parts of the book to itself or real life)
- How is the character in this book like another character?
- In which part of the story does the character seem happiest?
- Would you be insulted or complimented if someone said you were like the character? Why?
- Do you think the world would be a better place if everyone acted like the character?

Questions That Analyze (i.e., that break the subject into parts and explain each part)
- Who are the characters in the story?
- How is the setting different in the second half of the story?
- How does (the character's) mood change throughout the story?
- What are some things the characters have in common?
- What problem does the character have?

Questions That Synthesize (i.e., that apply knowledge to what is known and generate new ideas)
- Did the character do what you expected him or her to do? Explain.
- How do you think the character will solve the problem?

Questions That Evaluate (i.e., that give an opinion of the value of the subject)
- How do you think this book compares to the one we read last week?
- Which book do you think is the best one written by this author? Why?
- Do you think this would be a good book to give as a gift? Why or why not?

Questions Good Readers Ask

Questions about the Main Idea
- What is the story about?
- What is the problem?
- How will it be (or was it) solved?
- What do I need to know more about?

Questions about the Events of the Story
- What is going to happen next?
- Do I need to change my prediction?

Questions to Get a Clear Picture in My Mind
- What does this character (or thing) look like?
- What does the setting look like?

Questions to Summarize
- What has happened so far?
- Who did what?

Questions to Clarify
- Would it help to go back and reread that last part?
- Should I ignore and read on? Why?

Story Sequence

Draw a picture of what happened at the beginning, middle, and end of the story.

Beginning	**Middle**	**End**

The Kissing Hand

by Audrey Penn
(CHILD & FAMILY PRESS)

The Kissing Hand is about Chester Raccoon who is hesitant to start school. His mother assures him that he will enjoy school and everything new that comes with it. She gives him a family secret—a kissing hand. She kisses his hand, and anytime he needs to feel her love, he can press his hand against his cheek.

Phonemic Awareness

Phoneme Blending

Break down each of the following words from the story into phonemes: *him, if, at, and, fan, up, not, jump,* and *hand.* Hold a rubber band with two hands. As you say each sound (e.g., /h/ /i/ /m/), stretch apart the rubber band. Have children combine the phonemes to form the word (e.g., *him*). As they say the word, bring the two ends of the rubber band together. Then have children say each sound with you, and blend the sounds together to say the word again. Repeat this activity with each word.

Phonics

Consonant Digraph *sh*

Give several examples of words that include the consonant digraph *sh.* Write the story words *she, show,* and *wash* on the board. Invite children to read the words with you as they listen for the /sh/ sound. Read the following words aloud: *kiss, watch, fish, stop, shirt, chip, shop, wish, sip, ship,* and *wish.* Ask children to put a thumb up if the word contains the /sh/ sound or a thumb down if it does not. If the word contains the consonant digraph *sh,* write the word on the board and ask a volunteer to underline the digraph. Then read the word together with the class. Challenge children to think of other words with *sh* at the beginning, middle, or end. Give each child a copy of the Consonant Digraph *sh* reproducible (page 22) for more practice.

Repeated Exposure

Vocabulary

The Kissing Hand uses the concept of *warmth* to indicate emotion rather than temperature. The words *warmth* or *warm* are used in the following sentences in the book:

> "I know a wonderful secret that will make your nights at school seem as *warm* and cozy as your days at home."
>
> "Even his silky, black mask tingled with a special *warmth*."
>
> "And that very kiss will jump to your face and fill you with toasty *warm* thoughts."
>
> "The *warmth* of Chester's kiss filled her heart with special words."

Read aloud each of the sentences from the book, and ask children what they think the words *warmth* and *warm* mean as they are used. After discussing the concept of emotional warmth, use the words *warmth* and *warm* several times throughout the day to emphasize this concept. Challenge children to use these two words correctly in a sentence.

Read-Around

Fluency

After reading *The Kissing Hand* to children, photocopy and cut apart one set of the Read-Around cards (page 23) per group of children. If needed, preteach the following story words that are used in this activity: *hand, kiss, warm, love,* and *home.* Follow the directions for how to play the game (see page 7).

Answering Questions

Comprehension

Before reading the story, ask students *What do you think a kissing hand is?* Ask them to listen carefully as you read aloud the story to determine what a kissing hand is and why Chester Raccoon needed one. After reading the story, have children answer the questions and discuss their apprehensions about starting school and being separated from their parents.

Consonant Digraph sh

Write **sh** to complete each word.

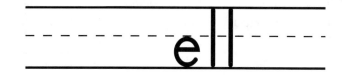

ell

ip

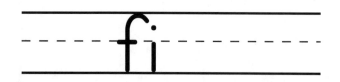

fi

bru

ovel

ark

Teaching Reading Using Picture Books • K–1 © 2005 Creative Teaching Press

Read-Around

I have   the first card.
Who has the word   **hand**?

I have the word   **hand.**
Who has the word   **kiss**?

I have the word   **kiss.**
Who has the word   **warm**?

I have the word   **warm.**
Who has the word   **love**?

I have the word   **love.**
Who has the word   **home**?

I have the word   **home.**
Who has   the first card?

The Apple Pie Tree

by Zoe Hall
(SCHOLASTIC)

The Apple Pie Tree is about two sisters who describe the changes their apple tree goes through during the seasons. The story ends with an apple pie being taken out of the oven.

Phonemic Awareness

Phoneme Isolation

Have children identify the beginning sound in each of the following words from the book: *apple, pie, winter, spring, nest, flower, just, blow, rains,* and *tree*. For example, ask children *What is the first sound you hear in* **apple**? Children should respond by saying *The first sound in* **apple** *is /a/*.

Phonics

Plural *s*

Draw on the board or on chart paper the chart below, leaving the second column blank for children to fill in. For each word, say the following sentences:

   I have one **apple**.
   I have two _____. (apples)

Ask children to help you determine the plural form of each word, and write it in the second column on the chart. When the chart is complete, ask them if they can see anything that the words in the second column have in common (the *s* at the end of each word.) Explain that adding an *s* to the end of a word shows that there is more than one (i.e., the word is plural). Give each child a Plural *s* reproducible (page 26) to provide more practice with plurals.

One	Two
apple	apples
robin	robins
bud	buds
egg	eggs
flower	flowers
blossom	blossoms
feather	feathers
petal	petals

Using Reference Books

Vocabulary

During circle time, introduce children to the dictionary. Explain that a dictionary can help you find the meaning of words and figure out how to spell words. Show children that the words in the dictionary are in alphabetical order. Look up the following words: *bare, guarding, buds, blossoms, brim*, or any words children are unfamiliar with from the book. Read the definition. Then, to aid understanding, read from the book the sentence containing the word. To check for understanding, ask children if they can use the word in a sentence.

Read-Around

Fluency

After you have read *The Apple Pie Tree* to the class, photocopy and cut apart one set of the Read-Around cards (page 27) per group of children. If needed, preteach the story words or phrases that are included in this activity: *brown winter tree, wind, bird nests, apples*, and *apple pie*. Follow the directions for how to play the game (see page 7).

Summarizing

Comprehension

After you have read aloud the book several times, ask the class to help write a summary of what happened to the apple tree in each season. On chart paper or on a whiteboard, write *Apple Tree*. Ask children what they can recall about the tree in the story. Write their answers on the board to summarize the events of each season. Use sequencing words for summarizing (e.g., *first, next, then, finally*) when you write their answers. Invite children to draw pictures next to each sentence.

APPLE TREE

First, the tree is brown and bare.

Then, leaves grow on every tiny branch.

Next, pink flower buds open.

Plural s

Copy the word, and add **s** to write the plural.

apple

_____
- - - - - - - - - - - - - - -
_____

cat

_____
- - - - - - - - - - - - - - -
_____

bird

_____
- - - - - - - - - - - - - - -
_____

flower

_____
- - - - - - - - - - - - - - -
_____

Teaching Reading Using Picture Books • K–1 © 2005 Creative Teaching Press

Read-Around

I have the first card.
Who has the **brown winter tree**?

I have the **brown winter tree**.
Who has the **wind**?

I have the **wind**.
Who has the **bird nests**?

I have the **bird nests**.
Who has the **apples**?

I have the **apples**.
Who has the **apple pie**?

I have the **apple pie**.
Who has the first card?

Red Leaf, Yellow Leaf

by Lois Ehlert

(HARCOURT)

Red Leaf, Yellow Leaf is about the life cycle of a sugar maple. It follows the tree from seed to the nursery to a boy's home where it changes with the seasons.

Phonemic Awareness

Phoneme Categorization

Have children pick out the word, from a set of three words, that has a different sound in a particular place. For example, say *Which word in this set does not belong: tree, twirled, boat?* Children should respond by saying **Boat**, *because it does not begin with /t/*. Repeat the activity with the following sets of words:

was, ground, **w**oods (ground)
t**win**e, mar**ked**, wra**pped** (twine)
unti**l**, snow, ba**ll** (snow)
fall, **f**avorite, come (come)
window, **s**ummer, **s**eeds (window)
Dad, **b**ed, **g**ot (got)
sn**ow**, year, sh**ow** (year)

Phonics

Long *e* with the Letters *ee*

Write the letters *ee* on the board. Tell children that when they see two *e*'s together in a word, they make the sound of long *e*. Write on the board each of the following words from the book: *tree, seeds, sleep, peek,* and *green*. Have children help you sound out each word and read it. Give each child a copy of the Long *e* with the Letters *ee* reproducible (page 30) to provide more practice with this long *e* pattern.

ee	
tree	peek
seeds	green
sleep	

Using Word Parts

Vocabulary

Write the prefix *un-* on the board. Explain to the class that this is a common prefix. Tell them that the prefix *un-* means "not" or "the opposite of." Write the word *unfold* on the board, and say the word aloud. Take a piece of paper and fold it in half. Say *This is how I **fold** a piece of paper.* Ask a volunteer to take the paper and show how to unfold the paper. Explain that adding *un-* to the beginning of the word changes the meaning. Read from the book the sentence containing the word *unfolded*: *"Tiny leaves unfolded on the stems."* Discuss the process that leaves go through as they are coming out of buds in the spring. Ask children to pretend to be leaves bunched up inside a bud and then to unfold.

Read-Around

Fluency

After reading the book to the class, photocopy and cut apart one set of the Read-Around cards (page 31) per group of children. If needed, preteach any of the following story words that are included in this activity: *seeds, sun, tree, red, yellow,* and *fall.* Follow the directions for how to play the game (see page 7).

Generating Questions

Comprehension

Before reading aloud *Red Leaf, Yellow Leaf,* tell children you would like them to raise their hand at any time during the reading to ask questions they might have about the text. Model the types of questions children may ask (e.g., *What does a particular word mean? What happens to the seeds?*). Read the story slowly, stopping to write down each question that is asked. (It may be helpful to have an aide or other adult write the questions down for you.) After you have finished, go back through each of the questions and have children help you answer them. Reread the book to reinforce the new words and concepts that were learned.

Long e with the Letters ee

Write **ee** to complete each word.

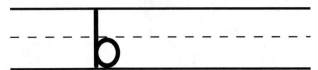

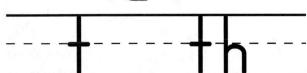

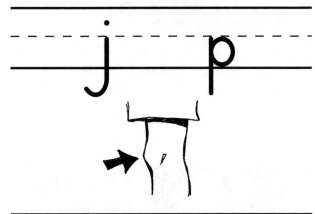

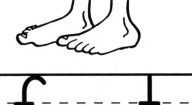

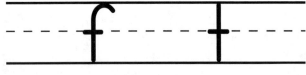

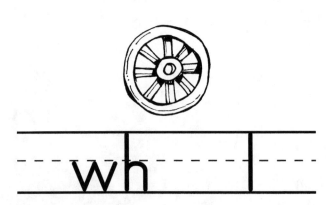

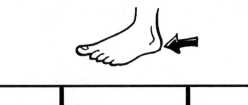

Teaching Reading Using Picture Books • K–1 © 2005 Creative Teaching Press

Read-Around

I have   the first card.
Who has   the **seeds**?

I have   the **seeds**.
Who has   the **sun**?

I have   the **sun**.
Who has   the **tree**?

I have   the **tree**.
Who has the **colors**   **red** and **yellow**?

I have the **colors**   **red** and **yellow**.
Who has   **fall**?

I have   **fall**.
Who has   the first card?

Where the Wild Things Are

by Maurice Sendak
(HARPERCOLLINS)

In *Where the Wild Things Are*, Max causes mischief, so he is sent to bed without supper. Luckily, a forest grows in his room, and he sails away to an adventure where the wild things are. Homesick, he returns to find his supper waiting for him.

Phonemic Awareness

Phoneme Addition

Have children add sounds to words from the book to create new words. For example, say *If you added /h/ to the beginning of **and**, what word would you have?* Children will respond by saying **Hand**. Repeat the activity with the following exercises:

Add /c/ to the beginning of *up.* (cup)   Add /w/ to the beginning of *all.* (wall)

Add /h/ to the beginning of *eat.* (heat)   Add /p/ to the beginning of *out.* (pout)

Add /b/ to the beginning of *room.* (broom)   Add /f/ to the beginning of *in.* (fin)

Phonics

Long and Short *o*

Draw on the board or on chart paper the chart below (without the words listed under the column titles). Review with the class the sounds that long and short *o* make. Read each of the following words from the story: *go, boat, across, lonely, almost, ocean, over, stop, no, hot, showed,* and *most.* Ask children to help you identify the sound in each as a long or short *o*. Write the words in the appropriate column on the chart. Give each child a copy of the Long and Short *o* reproducible (page 34) for more practice with the long and short *o* sounds.

Long o	Short o
go	across
boat	stop
lonely	hot
almost	
ocean	
over	
no	
showed	
most	

Using Context Clues

Vocabulary

As the story is read aloud, children might not be familiar with the words *mischief*, *private*, *gnashed*, *tamed*, and *rumpus*. Stop reading when you encounter one of these words, and ask children to look closely at the illustrations for clues about the meaning of the word. Also, encourage children to look for any clues in the sentence or surrounding sentences. Remind children that looking for clues can be a great way to figure out the meanings of words they may not be familiar with. Finally, have children act out the different words (e.g., have them act like wild animals and then *tamed* animals, *gnash* their teeth when they eat, or have a *rumpus* at recess).

Read-Around

Fluency

After reading aloud *Where the Wild Things Are*, photocopy and cut apart one set of the Read-Around cards (page 35) per group of children. If needed, preteach the following story words that are included in this activity: *boy*, *Max*, *night*, *boat*, *wild things*, and *king*. Follow the directions for how to play the game (see page 7).

Answering Questions

Comprehension

After reading the story to children, ask them the questions listed below. Reread the story to confirm their answers and to look for answers to the questions they may not have been able to answer.

1. Why did Max's mom call him a wild thing?
2. What was Max's punishment?
3. Do you think a forest really grew in Max's room?
4. Why did Max give up being king of where the wild things are?
5. What happens at the end of the story?

Long and Short o

Say the name of each picture. If you hear the **short o** sound, color the picture. If you hear the **long o** sound, draw a circle around the picture.

nose

goat

sock

bone

log

note

pot

toe

frog

Teaching Reading Using Picture Books • K–1 © 2005 Creative Teaching Press

Read-Around

I have   the first card.
Who has the **boy**   **Max**?

I have the **boy**   **Max**.
Who has the word   **night**?

I have the word   **night**.
Who has   the **boat**?

I have   the **boat**.
Who has   the **wild things**?

I have   the **wild things**.
Who has   the **king**?

I have   the **king**.
Who has   the first card?

Teaching Reading Using Picture Books • K–1 © 2005 Creative Teaching Press

Corduroy

by Don Freeman
(VIKING)

Corduroy is about a small bear who dreams of leaving the toy department of a large department store. One night, he leaves the toy department and ventures through the store in search of his missing button. The next day, he is purchased and taken home by a young girl.

Phonemic Awareness

Phoneme Identification

Ask children to identify the same sound or sounds in different words from the story. For example say *Which sound is the same in **wide**, **bed**, and **did**?* Children should respond by saying *The last sound, /d/, is the same.* Then challenge children to think of another word with the same sound. Repeat the activity with the following sets of words:

Mommy, piggy, very
lost, must, last
up, pop, lamp
waited, with, want
bear, button, big
how, him, home

Phonics

Long and Short *i*

Make a two-column chart on the board or on chart paper. Label the first column *Long i* and the second column *Short i*. Read the following words aloud: *tired, cried, pick, like, it, with, tight, in, right,* and *did.* Have the class guide you in writing the words in the proper column of the chart based on the vowel sounds. Give each child a Long and Short *i* reproducible (page 38) to provide more practice with the long and short *i* sounds.

Long i	Short i
tired	pick
cried	it
like	with
tight	in
right	did

Extended Instruction

After reading the story to the class, ask children if they know what a *department store* is. Give them examples of several department stores in your area, and explain that department stores have different areas, or departments, for items that are similar. Talk about the items you might find in the children's department or the furniture department. Ask children to think about what department they would like to work in. Each child may draw a picture of it and share it with the class or simply tell which department and why he or she would like to work there.

Read-Around

After reading the story to the children, photocopy and cut apart one set of the Read-Around cards (page 39) per group of children. If needed, preteach the following story words that are included in this activity: *bear, Corduroy, toy store, button, bed, girl,* and *Lisa.* Follow the directions for how to play the game (see page 7).

Generating Questions

After reading aloud the story a couple of times, divide the class into small groups. Ask each group to think of questions to ask the other groups about the story. Bring the class together, and have each group ask their questions to the rest of the class. If necessary, refer back to the book to find the answers.

Long and Short i

Say the name of each picture. If you hear the **short i** sound, color the picture.
If you hear the **long i** sound, draw a circle around the picture.

bike

fish

five

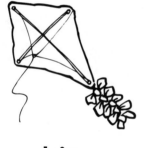

kite

iron

hill

ice

pig

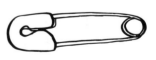

pin

Teaching Reading Using Picture Books • K–1 © 2005 Creative Teaching Press

Read-Around

I have   the first card.
Who has the **bear**   **Corduroy**?

I have the **bear**   **Corduroy**.
Who has   the **toy store**?

I have   the **toy store**.
Who has   the **button**?

I have   the **button**.
Who has   the **bed**?

I have   the **bed**.
Who has the **girl**   **Lisa**?

I have the **girl**   **Lisa**.
Who has   the first card?

Stone Soup

by Marcia Brown
(ATHENEUM BOOKS)

Stone Soup is a tale of three soldiers coming home from war. Tired and hungry, they stop in a village hoping to find food and shelter. The soldiers trick the greedy villagers into making them a feast.

Phonemic Awareness

Phoneme Addition

Have children add sounds to words from the book to create new words. For example, ask children *If you added /c/ to the beginning of* **up**, *what word would you have?* Children will respond by saying **Cup**. Repeat the activity with the following exercises:

Add /s/ to the beginning of *pot*. (spot)   Add /h/ to the beginning of *as*. (has)
Add /p/ to the beginning of *in*. (pin)   Add /b/ to the beginning of *ran*. (bran)
Add /t/ to the beginning of *all*. (tall)   Add /n/ to the beginning of *eat*. (neat)
Add /f/ to the beginning of *it*. (fit)   Add /b/ to the beginning of *us*. (bus)

Phonics

Sounds of *s*

Make a three-column chart on the board or on chart paper. Label the columns /s/, /z/, and /s/ *and* /z/. Write on sticky notes the story words listed below, and give the notes to the children. Explain that some of the words have the /s/ sound, some have the /z/ sound, and some words contain both sounds. Ask children to read aloud their word. Invite the whole class to decide which column the word should be placed in, based on the sound the *s* makes. Have children place their sticky note in the correct column. Give each child a copy of the Sounds of s reproducible (page 42) for more practice with the s sounds.

/s/ — sacks, strange, impossible, lights, soup
/z/ — wars, days, used, cabbages, easy, potatoes
/s/ and /z/ — soldiers, stones, themselves, ourselves, peasants

Preteaching Vocabulary

Without showing the pictures, read from the story the sentences in which the words *loft* and *cellar* are used. Ask children if they know what a *loft* and a *cellar* are. Have children draw a picture of what they think each one looks like. Then show children the pictures of the lofts and cellars in the book to show them what they actually look like.

Fluency

Read-Around

After reading the story to children, photocopy and cut apart one set of the Read-Around cards (page 43) per group of children. If needed, preteach the following story words used in this activity: *hungry, soldiers, three, stones, stone soup, big, pot,* and *milk*. Follow the directions for how to play the game (see page 7).

Comprehension

Answering Questions

Before reading the story to children a second time, read aloud a few of the questions listed below, and tell children to raise their hand when they hear an answer in the story. Invite a child to share the answer, and then raise a new question. Feel free to ask the questions during different readings. The questions below are listed in chronological order:

1. What did the peasants do when they heard the soldiers were coming? (hid their food)
2. Why did Paul and Francoise say they had no food? (because it had been a poor harvest)
3. What excuse did all of the peasants use for not having any food to share? (too many mouths to fill)
4. What kind of soup did the soldiers want to make? (stone soup)
5. What did the soldiers get first to make stone soup? (a large pot)
6. What did they do with the pot? (filled it with water and put it on the fire to boil)
7. How many stones did they need? (three)
8. What were the first three ingredients in the soup, after the stones? (salt, pepper, and carrots)
9. Where did Marie get the cabbages? (in the cupboard under the bed)
10. Who did the soldiers say they had made stone soup for? (the King)
11. What did the peasants bring to go with the soup? (bread, roast, and cider)
12. What did they do after they ate? (danced and sang)
13. Whose houses did the soldiers sleep in? (the priest's, the baker's, and the mayor's)
14. What did the peasants thank the soldiers for? (teaching them how to make stone soup)
15. What lesson did the peasants really learn? (cooperation and sharing)

Sounds of s

Say the name of each picture. If you hear the /s/ sound, color the picture.
If you hear the /z/ sound, draw a circle around the picture.

slide

six

fries

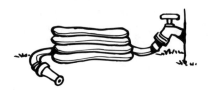

hose

goose

leaves

star

stop

rose

Teaching Reading Using Picture Books • K–1 © 2005 Creative Teaching Press

Read-Around

I have   the first card.
Who has   the **hungry soldiers**?

I have   the **hungry soldiers**.
Who has   **three stones**?

I have   **three stones**.
Who has   **stone soup**?

I have   **stone soup**.
Who has   a **big pot**?

I have   a **big pot**.
Who has   the **milk**?

I have   the **milk**.
Who has   the first card?

The Snowy Day

by Ezra Jack Keats
(VIKING)

The Snowy Day begins when a young boy awakens to find a winter wonderland. The boy has many adventures as he explores the snow-covered landscape.

Phonemic Awareness

Phoneme Isolation

Have children recognize individual sounds in a word. Ask children to identify the first sound in each of the following words from the story: *pointing, took, snowy, his,* and *woke.* Then ask children to come up with other words that start with that same sound.

Phonics

-ing Ending

Write on sentence strips or large cards the following base words: *walk, point, stick, smack, heap,* and *fall.* Read them with children several times until children are familiar with the words. On a separate sentence strip or card, write *ing.* Give one base word card to a volunteer, and the *ing* card to another volunteer. Have the two volunteers stand on opposite sides of the room (the base word to the left of children and the *ing* to the right). Have them read their cards while walking toward each other until they meet and the word comes together in the center of the room. Give each child a copy of the *-ing* Ending reproducible (page 46) to provide more practice.

Preteaching Vocabulary

Vocabulary

Before reading the story to the class, discuss the words below from the story. Have volunteers create a sentence for each word and act out their sentence.

sank — ". . . his feet *sank* into the snow." (page 10)

dragged — ". . . he *dragged* his feet slowly . . ." (page 12)

smacking — ". . . that was just right for *smacking* a snow-covered tree." (page 15)

heaping — ". . . a great big *heaping* mountain of snow . . ." (page 22)

Read-Around

Fluency

After reading *The Snowy Day* to the class, photocopy and cut apart one set of the Read-Around cards (page 47) per group of children. If needed, preteach the following story words that are included in this activity: *boy, Peter, snow, white, snowballs,* and *stick.* Follow the directions for how to play the game (see page 7).

Using Graphic Organizers

Comprehension

After reading the story several times, draw on the board the following web. Ask children to help you complete the web by recalling what Peter did in the snow. Refer back to the story to check your answers.

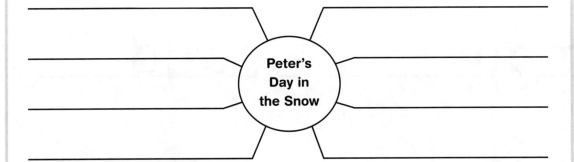

Peter's Day in the Snow

-ing Ending

Write **ing** to complete each word.

kick

play

smell

read

lick

yell

Teaching Reading Using Picture Books • K–1 © 2005 Creative Teaching Press

Read-Around

I have   the first card.
Who has the **boy**   **Peter**?

I have the **boy**   **Peter**.
Who has   **snow**?

I have   **snow**.
Who has the **color**   **white**?

I have the **color**   **white**.
Who has   **snowballs**?

I have   **snowballs**.
Who has   a **stick**?

I have   a **stick**.
Who has   the first card?

Froggy Gets Dressed

by Jonathan London
(VIKING)

In *Froggy Gets Dressed*, Froggy wakes up from his winter slumber to find snow. He gets dressed and goes outside to play until his mother reminds him to put on an article of clothing that he forgot. He repeats this on-again, off-again addition of clothing until he is too tired and goes back to bed.

Phonemic Awareness

Phoneme Blending

Break into phonemes (e.g., /p/ /a/ /n/ /t/ /s/) each of the following words from the story: *cold, went, melts, put, hat, flop,* and *left.* Use linking cubes as a visual for each phoneme. For example, for the word *pants*, have five cubes linked together. As you say each phoneme, take one cube away from the stack. Then have children combine the phonemes to form the word. As they combine the phonemes, link the cubes together.

Phonics

The Letter *z*

Write on the board the letter *z*, and ask children what sound it makes. Read one of the pages showing Froggy getting dressed, and stress the words that begin with the letter *z* (e.g., "So Froggy put on his socks — *zoop!* Pulled on his boots — *zup!* Put on his hat — *zap!* Tied on his scarf — *zwit!* Tugged on his mittens — *zum!*"). Ask children if these *z* words are real or made up. Explain that they are made-up words used to represent a sound effect. Give each child a piece of paper and crayons. Invite children to draw themselves putting on one item of clothing and to make up a word beginning with the letter *z* to represent the sound of putting on the item. Have children write or dictate a sentence to go with their picture and sound-effect word (e.g., Grace put on her coat — *zoog!*). Give each child a copy of The Letter *z* reproducible (page 50) to provide more practice.

Grace put on her coat - Zoog!

Using Reference Books

Show children a thesaurus, and explain that it is a book used to find words with the same meaning. Ask children what they think the story word *flopped* means; then look up the root word *flop* in the thesaurus. Replace the word *flopped* in the story with the synonyms found in the thesaurus. Have children act out the word to reinforce the meaning.

Fluency

Read-Around

After reading *Froggy Gets Dressed* to the class, photocopy and cut apart one set of the Read-Around cards (page 51) per group of children. If needed, preteach any of the story words used in this activity: *socks*, *boots*, *hat*, *pants*, and *coat*. Follow the directions for how to play the game (see page 7).

Comprehension

Using Graphic Organizers

Draw on the board or on chart paper the story map below. Have children help you fill in each section and complete it. When you are finished, reread the story to be sure you have remembered everything.

Title _____

Author _____

Characters _____

Setting _____

Somebody (the main character or characters)

_____

Wanted (what the main character is trying to do)

_____

But (the problem the main character runs into)

_____

So (how the main character solves the problem)

_____

The Letter z

Write **z** under each picture that begins with the letter **z**.

_____

– – – – – – –

_____

_____

– – – – – – –

_____

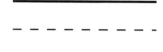

_____

– – – – – – –

_____

_____

– – – – – – –

_____

_____

– – – – – – –

_____

_____

– – – – – – –

_____

_____

– – – – – – –

_____

_____

– – – – – – –

_____

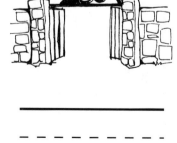

_____

– – – – – – –

_____

Teaching Reading Using Picture Books • K–1 © 2005 Creative Teaching Press

Read-Around

I have the first card.
Who has the **socks**?

I have the **socks**.
Who has the **boots**?

I have the **boots**.
Who has the **hat**?

I have the **hat**.
Who has the **pants**?

I have the **pants**.
Who has the **coat**?

I have the **coat**.
Who has the first card?

The Mitten

by Jan Brett
(G. P. Putnam's Sons)

The Mitten is a Ukrainian folktale about a boy who drops his white mitten in the snow. Animal after animal takes shelter in the stretched out mitten until the mouse's whiskers make the bear sneeze and all of the animals fly out.

Phonemic Awareness

Phoneme Substitution

Have children make a new word by substituting one phoneme for another. For example, ask *If we change the /l/ in **let** to /g/, what is the new word?* Children will respond by saying **Get**. Repeat the activity with the following words:

soon—Change /s/ to /m/. (moon)
but—Change /t/ to /g/. (bug)
wet—Change /w/ to /p/. (pet)
he—Change /h/ to /w/. (we)
big—Change /b/ to /p/. (pig)
room—Change /m/ to /t/. (root)
mitten—Change /m/ to /k/. (kitten)

Phonics

Consonant Digraph *wh*

Write on the board the following words from the story: *white, when, what,* and *whiskers*. Invite children to read aloud the words with you. Identify the beginning sound of the words, circling the *wh* in each word. Ask children to brainstorm other words beginning with *wh* (e.g., *whistle, wheel, whisper, while, where, whine, who, why*). Make a list of the new words. Give each child a copy of the Consonant Digraph *wh* reproducible (page 54) to provide more practice.

Vocabulary

Using Context Clues

Read from the story the pages where each of the animals listed below appears. As you read a page, put emphasis on the word or words listed below for each animal. Read the remainder of the page, and ask children to help you figure out what each word means by looking for clues in the text and pictures. After you have come up with the meaning of the word, move on to the next animal and corresponding word.

mole — *burrowed*
hedgehog — *jostled*
owl — *grumbled*
bear — *swelled, bulged*

Fluency

Read-Around

After reading the story to the class, photocopy and cut apart one set of the Read-Around cards (page 55) per group of children. If needed, preteach the following story words included in this activity: *white mittens*, *snow*, *mole*, *fox*, and *bear*. Follow the directions for how to play the game (see page 7).

Comprehension

Answering Questions

After children are familiar with the story, ask them to help you summarize the events that take place in the book. Explain that a summary gives the main points that happen in the story without giving many details. Have children stand in a line and take turns recalling the progression of the story. Encourage them to use sequencing words (e.g., *first, second, next, then, last, finally*) as they are recalling the main events. Write their sentences on the board. When you are finished, reread the summary to verify that all the main points are in the correct order.

First, the mitten fell in the snow.

Consonant Digraph wh

Write **wh** to complete each word.

____ a l e

____ e a t

____ e e l

____ i p

____ i s t l e

____ i t e

Teaching Reading Using Picture Books • K–1 © 2005 Creative Teaching Press

Read-Around

I have   the first card.
Who has   the **white mittens**?

I have   the **white mittens**.
Who has   the **snow**?

I have   the **snow**.
Who has   the **mole**?

I have   the **mole**.
Who has   the **fox**?

I have   the **fox**.
Who has   the **bear**?

I have   the **bear**.
Who has   the first card?

Arthur's Valentine

by Marc Brown
(LITTLE, BROWN AND COMPANY)

In *Arthur's Valentine*, Arthur receives a valentine from a secret admirer. He follows the clues to discover the identity of his admirer.

Phonemic Awareness

Phoneme Segmentation

Have children break into phonemes the words *box*, *hid*, *lips*, *ran*, *lunch*, *sang*, and *this*. Have children clap, tap, or stomp the number of phonemes as they say each one. For example, ask children *How many sounds can you hear in **and**?* Children will clap three times as they say /a/ /n/ /d/ — *three sounds*.

Phonics

Long and Short *e*

Tape two large pieces of paper to the board. Write *Long e* on one piece of paper, and write *Short e* on the other piece. Give examples of words containing the long *e* (e.g., *eat*, *eel*, *beep*) and short *e* (e.g., *best*, *elephant*, *wet*). Write on cards the following words from the story: *maybe*, *she*, *teasing*, *treat*, *sweet*, *Ellen*, *fell*, *everyone*, *instead*, and *pocket*. Hand out the cards to children, and ask them to read their word. Then have children determine which *e* sound they have and tape their card onto the correct piece of paper. Invite children to draw on the correct piece of paper pictures of words that have either a long or short *e*. Give each child a copy of the Long and Short *e* reproducible (page 58) to provide more practice.

Repeated Exposure

Before reading aloud the story, ask children if they know what a *secret admirer* is. Explain that a secret admirer is someone who really likes you a lot but doesn't want you to know who he or she is. Ask children if they can think of some ways secret admirers might tell you they like you without telling you who they are (e.g., writing letters, sending flowers). Write on small pieces of paper each child's name. Let each child choose a name, and ask him or her to draw a picture and sign it *From your secret admirer*. Ask children to find a way to secretly leave the picture for their friend without being seen. After everyone has received their picture, have children tell who they were a secret admirer to and how they left their picture without being seen.

Read-Around

After reading the literature selection to the class, photocopy and cut apart one set of the Read-Around cards (page 59) per group of children. If needed, preteach the following story words included in this activity: *boy*, *Arthur*, *card*, *box*, *movies*, and *candy kiss*. Follow the directions for how to play the game (see page 7).

Generating Questions

Tell children you are going to read aloud the story and that you would like them to see if they can come up with questions about what you read. Explain that you would like them to think of questions that might be tricky for the class to answer. Read the story, stopping at the end of each page to invite a child to ask a question. Encourage the other children to answer the question if they can. If they do not know the answer, reread the page to help them find it.

Long and Short e

Say the name of each picture. If you hear the **short e** sound, color the picture.
If you hear the **long e** sound, draw a circle around the picture.

leaf

bed

feet

key

pen

net

seal

tree

tent

Teaching Reading Using Picture Books • K–1 © 2005 Creative Teaching Press

Read-Around

I have   the first card.
Who has the **boy**   **Arthur**?

I have the **boy**   **Arthur**.
Who has   a **card**?

I have   a **card**.
Who has   a **box**?

I have   a **box**.
Who has   the **movies**?

I have   the **movies**.
Who has   a **candy kiss**?

I have   a **candy kiss**.
Who has   the first card?

Tacky the Penguin

by Helen Lester

(HOUGHTON MIFFLIN)

In *Tacky the Penguin*, Tacky is an odd bird. He does everything differently from the other penguins. This pays off when hunters come and his odd habits scare them away.

Phonemic Awareness

Phoneme Deletion

Ask children to identify the new word formed when a phoneme is deleted from a story word. For example, ask children *What is **ran** without /r/?* Children will respond by saying ***Ran** without /r/ is **an***. Repeat the activity using the following words:

hearty without /y/ (heart)

switch without /s/ (witch)

tacky without /y/ (tack)

slap without /s/ (lap)

lived without /d/ (live)

land without /l/ (and)

lovely without /ly/ (love)

Phonics

Consonant Digraphs *ch* and *sh*

Write on cards the story words *shared, splashy, fish, march, chanting, catch,* and *rich*. Give one card each to seven volunteers. Divide the remainder of the class in half, and assign one group /ch/ and the other /sh/. Ask the groups to say the sound of their consonant digraph. Invite each volunteer to read his or her word. If the word contains /sh/, the /sh/ group will make their sound. If the word has the /ch/ sound, the /ch/ group will make their sound. The children holding the cards will join the team that matched their sound. Add more word cards to give other children a turn. Give each child a copy of the Consonant Digraphs *ch* and *sh* reproducible (page 62) to provide more practice.

Preteaching Vocabulary

Before reading *Tacky the Penguin* to the class for the first time, write on the board each of the following vocabulary words: *odd, companions, politely, hearty, graceful, fright,* and *dreadful.* Ask children if they know what any of the words mean or if they can use any of them in a sentence. Give additional information about the words as needed. After children are familiar with the vocabulary words, provide practice using the words by inviting children to help you write a story that includes all of the words. The words may be used more than once, and different forms of the words (e.g., plurals) may be used. Next, read *Tacky the Penguin,* pausing at each of the vocabulary words to be sure children understand the meaning of the word within the context of the story.

Read-Around

After reading *Tacky the Penguin* to the children, photocopy and cut apart one set of the Read-Around cards (page 63) per group of children. If needed, preteach any of the following story words included in this activity: *odd bird, Tacky, ice, shirt,* and *hunters.* Follow the directions for how to play the game (see page 7).

Using Graphic Organizers

Draw on the board or on chart paper the chart below with only the column titles. Ask children to help you recall how Tacky was different than the other penguins. On the left side of the chart, list the actions of the other penguins; and on the right side, list the actions Tacky would perform instead. After you have finished, reread the story and have children listen for any comparisons they may have missed.

Penguins' Actions	Tacky's Actions
shook hands	slapped others on their back
marched in a straight line	jumped and rolled

Consonant Digraphs ch and sh

Say the name of each picture. If you hear the /ch/ sound, write **ch** to complete the
word. If you hear the /sh/ sound, write **sh** to complete the word.

___ fi ___

air

oe

cat

Iun

ip

Teaching Reading Using Picture Books • K–1 © 2005 Creative Teaching Press

Read-Around

I have	the first card.
Who has	an **odd bird**?

I have	an **odd bird**.
Who has	**Tacky**?

I have	**Tacky**.
Who has	the **ice**?

I have	the **ice**.
Who has	a **shirt**?

I have	a **shirt**.
Who has	the **hunters**?

I have	the **hunters**.
Who has	the first card?

Big Red Barn

by Margaret Wise Brown
(HarperCollins)

Big Red Barn is a simple story, set to rhymed text, of the different animals living together in a barnyard.

Phoneme Blending

Break into phonemes each of the following words from the story: *big, hen, pig, leg, and, ten, too, cat, dog,* and *sun.* Have children combine the phonemes to re-form each word. Then ask for volunteers. Assign each volunteer a phoneme (e.g., /b/, /i/, /g/). Have each volunteer stand in front of the class in the order that his or her phoneme appears in the word and say aloud his or her phoneme. Encourage volunteers to repeat their phoneme slightly faster each time to blend the sounds that make the word.

Phonics

The *-ay* Word Family

Explain that the vowel combination *ay* makes the long *a* sound. Write on the board the following words from the story: *away, today, play, day, hay,* and *bray.* Invite individual children to come up and underline the *ay.* Then have the class sound out the letters to say the word. Give each child a copy of The *-ay* Word Family reproducible (page 66) to provide more practice.

Vocabulary

Repeated Exposure

Write on separate cards each of the following animal sounds from the story: *squealed, lowed, bray,* and *squeaking.* Ask for a volunteer to demonstrate each sound. After children are familiar with the words, divide the class into four groups. Explain that you will show a card to each group and that they will respond by making the sound indicated on the card. Start out by slowly going through each card, and gradually increase the speed until your classroom sounds like a funny farm.

Fluency

Read-Around

After reading the story to the class, photocopy and cut apart one set of the Read-Around cards (page 67) per group of children. If needed, preteach any of the following story words or phrases that are included in this activity: *big red barn, pink pig, old black cat, big red dog,* and *brown cow.* Follow the directions for how to play the game (see page 7).

Comprehension

Monitoring Comprehension

Have a pad of sticky notes available as you read the story to the class for the first time. Explain to children that you would like them to raise their hand each time they hear a word or concept they do not understand. Each time a question arises, put a sticky note on the page, and write the question on it. Continue to read the story without answering the questions. After you have finished the story, go through and address each note. Have children help each other with their questions, and refer to reference aids if needed to answer all the questions. Remove each note as the question is answered. Reread the story without stopping.

The -ay Word Family

Write **ay** to complete each word.

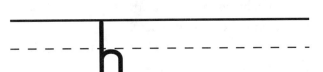
h____   cr____   ____on

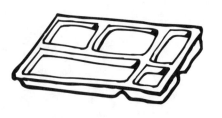

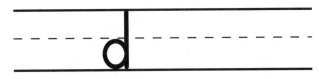
d____   p l____

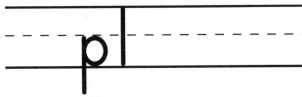

X-r____   tr____

Read-Around

I have   the first card.
Who has   the **big red barn**?

I have   the **big red barn**.
Who has   the **pink pig**?

I have   the **pink pig**.
Who has   the **old black cat**?

I have   the **old black cat**.
Who has   the **big red dog**?

I have   the **big red dog**.
Who has   the **brown cow**?

I have   the **brown cow**.
Who has   the first card?

Teaching Reading Using Picture Books • K–1 © 2005 Creative Teaching Press

Guess How Much I Love You

by Sam McBratney

(CANDLEWICK PRESS)

In *Guess How Much I Love You*, a parent rabbit and a child rabbit compare their immeasurable love for each other.

Phonemic Awareness

Phoneme Substitution

Have children make a new word by substituting one phoneme for another. For example, ask children *If we change the /b/ in* **bed** *to /r/, what is the new word?* Children will respond by saying **Red**. Repeat the activity using the following words:

big—Change /g/ to /b/. (bib)
long—Change /l/ to /s/. (song)
wish—Change /sh/ to /g/. (wig)
much—Change /m/ to /s/. (such)
feet—Change /t/ to /d/. (feed)
reach—Change /r/ to /t/. (teach)
him—Change /m/ to /p/. (hip)

Phonics

The *-own* Word Family

Write *brown* and *down* on the board, and underline *own* in each word. Have the class read aloud the words together. Invite children to brainstorm other words containing *own* in them (e.g., *drown, frown, gown, town, clown, crown, downtown*). Give each child a copy of The *-own* Word Family reproducible (page 70) to provide more practice.

Using Reference Books

Vocabulary

Write on the board the following sentence from the story:
*"I love you all the way down the **lane** as far as the river."* Read it aloud to children,
emphasizing the word *lane*. Look up the word in the dictionary, and read its definition
to your class. Invite children to replace *lane* with other words that the dictionary uses to
describe *lane*. Write on the board the new sentences, and then read aloud each sentence
to see if it makes sense.

Read-Around

Fluency

After reading the story to the children, photocopy and cut
apart one set of the Read-Around cards (page 71) per group of children. If needed,
preteach any of the following story words included in this activity: *little, big, hop, far,*
or *moon*. Follow the directions for how to play the game (see page 7).

Generating and Answering Questions

Comprehension

Divide your class into two teams, the "x's" and the "o's."
Ask each child to write on an index card a question about the story. Draw on the board
a large tic-tac-toe grid. Tape one question, facedown, in each box of the grid. Invite the
teams to take turns choosing a card and answering the question. Place an *x* or an *o* in
the box for the team that answers the question correctly. If neither team can answer
the question, find the answer in the book. Then put a new card in the box to replace
that question. Continue until a team wins. Play the game again with new cards, and
continue in this manner until all the questions have been answered.

The -own Word Family

Write **own** to complete each word.

do

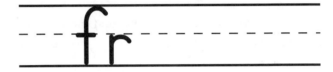

fr

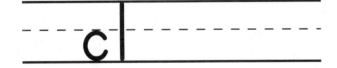

cl

cr

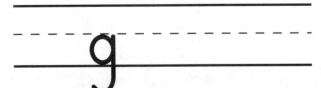

g

t

Read-Around

I have   the first card.
Who has the word   **little**?

I have the word   **little**.
Who has the word   **big**?

I have the word   **big**.
Who has the word   **hop**?

I have the word   **hop**.
Who has the word   **far**?

I have the word   **far**.
Who has the word   **moon**?

I have the word   **moon**.
Who has   the first card?

The Relatives Came

by Cynthia Rylant
(ATHENEUM/RICHARD
JACKSON BOOKS)

In *The Relatives Came*, a large group of relatives come to visit a family one summer. They have a great time together, and then the relatives return home sadly, but know they will see the family next summer.

Phoneme Addition

Phonemic Awareness

Have children add sounds to words from the book to create new words. For example, ask *If you added /p/ to the beginning of* **up**, *what word would you have?* Children respond by saying **Pup**. Repeat the activity with the following exercises:

Add /f/ to the beginning of *old*. (fold)   Add /g/ to the beginning of *ate*. (gate)

Add /s/ to the beginning of *it*. (sit)   Add /t/ to the end of *an*. (ant)

Add /b/ to the beginning of *us*. (bus)   Add /t/ to the end of *car*. (cart)

Add /h/ to the beginning of *all*. (hall)

Consonant Digraph *th*

Phonics

Draw on the board the chart below. Explain that the letters *th* can be found at the beginning, middle, or end of words. Write on index cards the following words from the story: *the, they, thought, their, three, them, those, with, through, clothes, things, together, breathing, three, then,* and *thrown*. Give the cards to children, and ask them to use a red crayon to underline *th* on their card. Then invite them to tape their card in the correct column on the chart. Give each child a copy of the Consonant Digraph *th* reproducible (page 74) to provide more practice.

Beginning th_____	Middle ____th____	End _____th

Preteaching Vocabulary

Vocabulary

Before reading the story to the class, discuss the meaning of the following phrases: *quiet talk*, *shining faces*, *tend to the garden*, and *came up from Virginia*. Have children give an explanation of what they think each phrase means before you tell them the meaning. After discussing these phrases, ask children if any of these phrases remind them of something they have done or have heard about. Discuss with children the similarities. Point out to children that this is called a *text connection*. To further reinforce the meaning of each phrase, write the phrases across the top of a piece of chart paper. Invite children to come up and draw a picture of what each phrase means.

I help my mom tend to the garden by pulling weeds.

Read-Around

Fluency

After reading the literature selection to the children, photocopy and cut apart one set of the Read-Around cards (page 75) per group of children. If needed, preteach any of the following story words that are used in this activity: *summer*, *relatives*, *car*, *hug*, or *bed*. Follow the directions for how to play the game (see page 7).

Monitoring Comprehension

Comprehension

Read the story, one page at a time, stopping at any words or concepts that you think children may not understand. Ask children to clarify the meanings of these words and concepts. For example, ask children what they think it means when the story says that to get to from the kitchen to the front room "you'd have to go through at least four different hugs." After the class understands everything on a page, go on to the next page. Continue in this fashion until you have finished the book. Reread the book without interruption.

Consonant Diagraph th

Write **th** to complete each word.

_____
_ _ _ _ _ _ _ _
r e e

_____
_ _ _ _ _ _ _ _
m a

_____
_ _ _ _ _ _ _ _
r o w

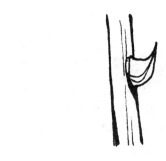
_____
_ _ _ _ _ _ _ _
o r n

_____
_ _ _ _ _ _ _ _
b a

_____
_ _ _ _ _ _ _ _
u m b

Teaching Reading Using Picture Books • K–1 © 2005 Creative Teaching Press

Read-Around

I have   the first card.
Who has   **summer**?

I have   **summer**.
Who has   the **relatives**?

I have   the **relatives**.
Who has   a **car**?

I have   a **car**.
Who has the word   **hug**?

I have the word   **hug**.
Who has   a **bed**?

I have   a **bed**.
Who has   the first card?

The Rainbow Fish

by Marcus Pfister
(NORTH-SOUTH BOOKS)

In *The Rainbow Fish*, a beautiful fish finds himself without friends because he will not share his shimmering scales. An octopus tells the fish that he will be happy if he shares. The fish follows the advice and finds happiness.

Phonemic Awareness

Phoneme Identification

Ask children to identify the same sound or sounds in different words from the story. For example, ask *Which sound is the same in **fish**, **splash** and **starfish**?* Children will respond by saying *The last sound, /sh/, is the same.* Repeat the activity using the following sets of words:

> **fish**, **splash**, **starfish**
> **there**, **the**, **they**
> **day**, **away**, **play**
> left, right, felt
> **sh**iny, **sh**immer, **sh**ocked
> **g**ive, **g**reen, **g**et
> flash**ing**, glimmer**ing**, lett**ing**
> **st**arfish, **st**arted, **st**ory

Phonics

sw Blend

Write on the board the words *swim* and *swam*, and then read them aloud with your class. Circle *sw* in both words, making the sound of the blend as you circle it. Invite children to brainstorm other words beginning with *sw*. Write these words on the board as well. Give each child a copy of the *sw* Blend reproducible (page 78) to provide more practice.

Repeated Exposure

Vocabulary

Point out the word *peculiar* in the story. Read the word in the context of the sentence. Discuss the meaning of *peculiar*, and then ask for a volunteer to make up a sentence using the word. Begin a list by writing at the top of a piece of chart paper the title *Peculiar Events*. Over the course of several days, invite children to dictate anything that happens at school that they find peculiar. Write their responses on the chart paper. At the end of the week, read through the list together.

> Peculiar Events
> 1. The recess bell didn't ring.
> 2. There hasn't been pizza for lunch in three days.
> 3.

Read-Around

Fluency

After reading *The Rainbow Fish* to children, photocopy and cut apart one set of the Read-Around cards (page 79) per group of children. If needed, preteach any of the following story words that are included in this activity: *sea, fish, shiny scales, share,* or *one.* Follow the directions for how to play the game (see page 7).

Summarizing

Comprehension

Describe what a summary is (i.e., the main points of the story in just a few words). Remind children that summaries should be brief. Make the analogy that a summary is like a tube of toothpaste—you only squeeze out what you need to get the job done and leave the rest in the tube. After reading the story several times, divide the class into small groups. Ask each group to draw a series of pictures that summarize the story. Have them write or dictate sentences to go with each picture. Invite each group to share their pictures with the rest of the class.

sw Blend

Write **sw** to complete each word.

———— im

———— an

———— eater

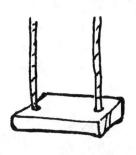

———— ing

———— eep

———— itch

Read-Around

I have the first card.
Who has the **sea**?

I have the **sea**.
Who has the **fish**?

I have the **fish**.
Who has **shiny scales**?

I have **shiny scales**.
Who has the word **share**?

I have the word **share**.
Who has the number **one**?

I have the number **one**.
Who has the first card?

Teaching Reading Using Picture Books • K–1 © 2005 Creative Teaching Press

 # Literature Selections

The following titles (listed alphabetically by author) are used in this book:

Brett, Jan
The Mitten
(G. P. Putnam's Sons)

Brown, Marc
Arthur's Valentine
(Little, Brown and Company)

Brown, Marcia
Stone Soup
(Atheneum Books)

Brown, Margaret Wise
Big Red Barn
(HarperCollins)

Ehlert, Lois
Red Leaf, Yellow Leaf
(Harcourt)

Freeman, Don
Corduroy
(Viking)

Hall, Zoe
The Apple Pie Tree
(Scholastic)

Keats, Ezra Jack
The Snowy Day
(Viking)

Lester, Helen
Tacky the Penguin
(Houghton Mifflin)

London, Jonathan
Froggy Gets Dressed
(Viking)

McBratney, Sam
Guess How Much I Love You
(Candlewick Press)

Penn, Audrey
The Kissing Hand
(Child & Family Press)

Pfister, Marcus
The Rainbow Fish
(North-South Books)

Rylant, Cynthia
The Relatives Came
(Atheneum/Richard Jackson Books)

Sendak, Maurice
Where the Wild Things Are
(HarperCollins)